A FUN BOOK OF MOVEM

JUMP ALO

This edition published 1992
by BCA by arrangement with
WAYLAND (PUBLISHERS) LTD

CN 5571

First published in 1990 by
Firefly Books Limited
61 Western Road, Hove
East Sussex BN3 1JD, England

Editor: Francesca Motisi

Typeset by DP Press Limited, Sevenoaks, Kent
Printed and bound in Belgium by Casterman S.A.

A FUN BOOK OF MOVEMENT

JUMP ALONG

Written by Neil Morris
Illustrated by Peter Stevenson

BCA
LONDON · NEW YORK · SYDNEY · TORONTO

Joe is a shy little kangaroo. He's always hiding away in his mother's pouch. While his cousins are jumping about, Joe stays with his mum.

'You're old enough now to
get around on your own,'
Mum says.
'But I can't jump!' Joe cries.

'Nonsense!' Joe's father shouts.
'All kangaroos can jump.'

With that he bounds off, and the others follow.

'I don't want to jump,' Joe says, closing his eyes.

Now poor Joe is sad.

'I've lost my family, because I didn't want to jump,' he tells the birds.

'Come and fly with us,' the birds twitter. Joe flaps his arms and his tail, but he doesn't take off.

'You can't be in our family if you don't fly,' the birds sing. Then they fly away.

'I'll teach you the best way to get around,' a snake hisses. 'Slither along with me!'

'It feels uncomfortable,' Joe tells the snake.

'It looks ridiculous!' the snake sniggers and slithers away.

'You could make a useful elephant,' a loud voice booms. 'We stomp all over the place. Would you like to stomp along?'

Joe stamps his feet, but he hardly moves.

'I can't stomp so fast,' he shouts.

‘Whatever can I do?’ Joe wonders.

‘We swim about in the water all day,’ a little fish splutters. ‘Come in, it’s easy!’

Joe wiggles his tail, like the fish. But he doesn’t swim, he sinks.

‘He can’t be with us if he can’t swim,’ the fish chant.

‘You’re just like my ducklings – scared of water!’ a mother duck quacks. ‘Get in the queue and waddle along with us.’

The ducklings don’t like the look of Joe.

‘He’s not waddling properly,’ they tell their mother.

‘Waddling will get you nowhere fast,’ a tiger growls. ‘Come on the prowl with me.’

‘Am I prowling properly?’ Joe asks. But the tiger has prowled off on his own.

‘Never trust a tiger!’ a little monkey calls. ‘Climb up to us.’

The monkey shows Joe how to climb the tree, but Joe keeps slipping down.

‘I can’t climb,’ Joe cries.

'You knocked?' a mole asks. 'Come on down. Just burrow!' Joe tries his best.

'You have to dig much harder,' the mole orders. 'We moles burrow all day and night.'

‘I’ll never find a family to get along with,’ the little kangaroo thinks.

‘You wouldn’t have liked it down there, it’s too dark,’ a beetle says. ‘It’s better to crawl on top.’

‘But you’re not crawling, you’re hopping,’ the beetle complains.

‘Hopping is fun!’ Joe says.

‘Not for me,’ says the beetle, and crawls off.

'It's a pity no one else likes leaping,' says Joe.

'Well, you could never keep up with me,' Frog croaks. 'We frogs are the best!'

The little kangaroo jumps much further than the boastful frog.

'I can jump,' Joe shouts. 'Look at me, I can jump!'

Joe jumps, hops and leaps along.
'I can jump like a kangaroo!' he cries.

‘Of course you can,’ Joe’s father says.
‘All kangaroos can jump. Jump along!’

Discussion points

This book encourages children to think about different kinds of movement. It might also help to give some understanding of the animal world. Doing something for the first time requires courage and you can help your child overcome his/her worries by showing understanding and praising his/her skills.

4/5 Joe's cousins enjoy jumping about, but why is Joe hiding away? Have you ever been frightened of doing something your friends enjoyed?
Can frogs jump?

6/7 Joe has fallen out of his mother's pouch. Will anyone come back for him? How far can you jump? Put some cushions on the floor and see!

8/9 Frog has come back. He likes a bit of fun.
Joe wants to fly like a bird, but he hasn't got wings.
Frog has a good idea, but two feathers don't make a bird!

10/11 Try slithering across the room. Is it a good way of moving around?

12/13 When you stamp your feet, you make a lot of noise.

14/15 Fish can swim under water, but Joe wouldn't be able to stay under for long because he can't breathe under water.
Have you learnt to swim yet?

16/17 Big webbed feet are good for waddling, and even better for paddling.
Why don't the ducklings like Joe?

18/19 Get down on your hands and knees and pretend to to be a tiger prowling through the jungle. It's quite difficult. Joe is not all that good at it, is he?

20/21 Who are the best climbers in this picture?
Do you like climbing?

22/23 How many animals do you know that live underground? (rabbits, badgers, moles, etc.)

24/25 Joe has tried lots of different ways of getting about. Suddenly he discovers that he loves hopping. Hopping is fun and easy for a kangaroo.

26/27 Joe is very pleased with his leaps. Frog is annoyed. Do you know why?

28/29 Joe is happy because he can jump like a kangaroo. Imagine you were frightened of walking on two feet and suddenly found that it is easy to walk. You would be pleased too.

30/31 Joe's father always knew that Joe would turn into an expert jumper.
So next time you are worried about running, skipping or even jumping, think of Joe and 'Jump Along!'